Copyright © 2017 Honey Badger
All rights reserved.

FREE DOWNLOAD!

www.honeybadgercoloring.com/fresh

YOUR DOWNLOAD CODE: FF3928

@honeybadgercoloring

Honey Badger Coloring

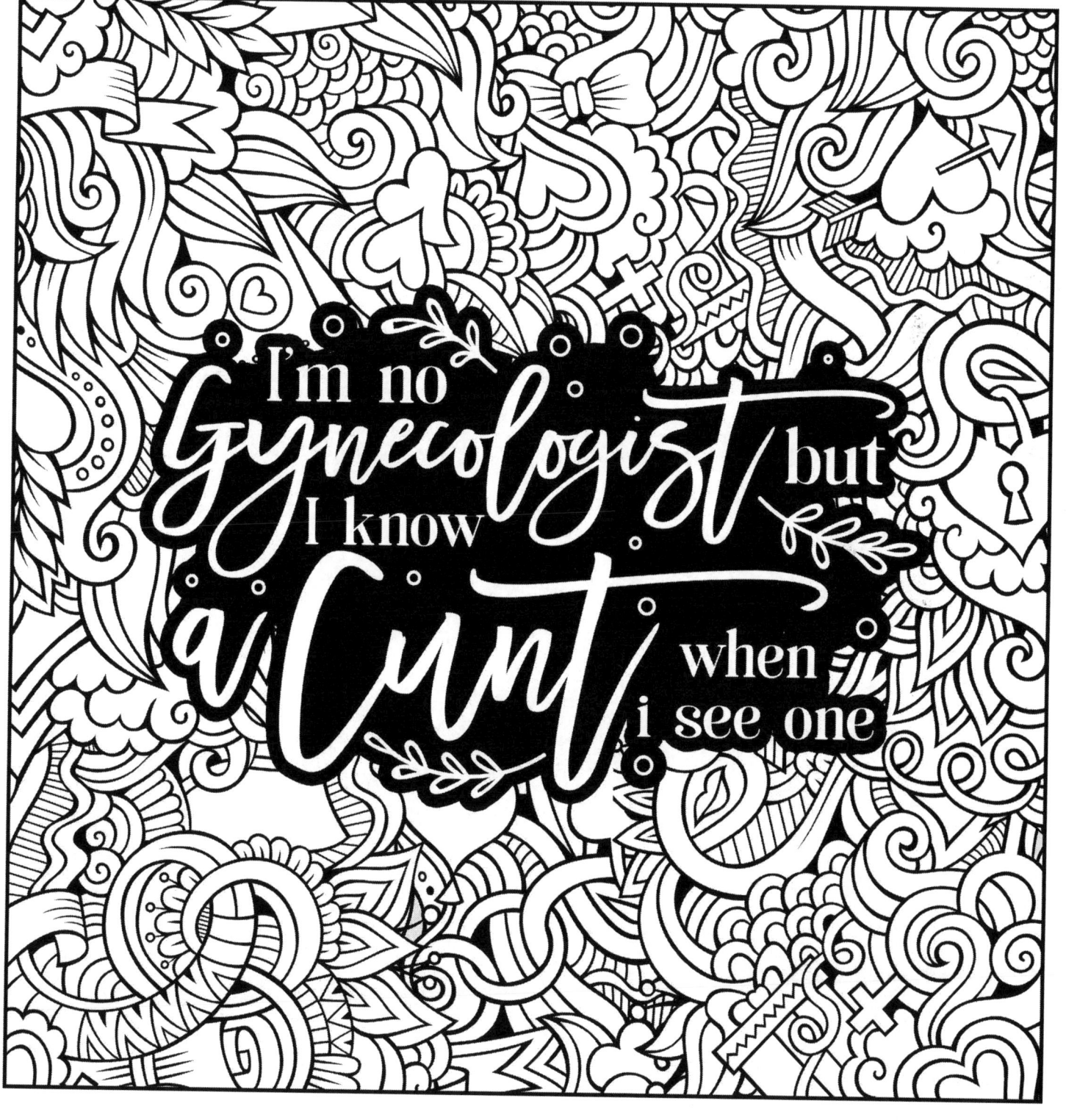

I'm not good with apologies so GO UNFUCK YOURSELF ...or whatever

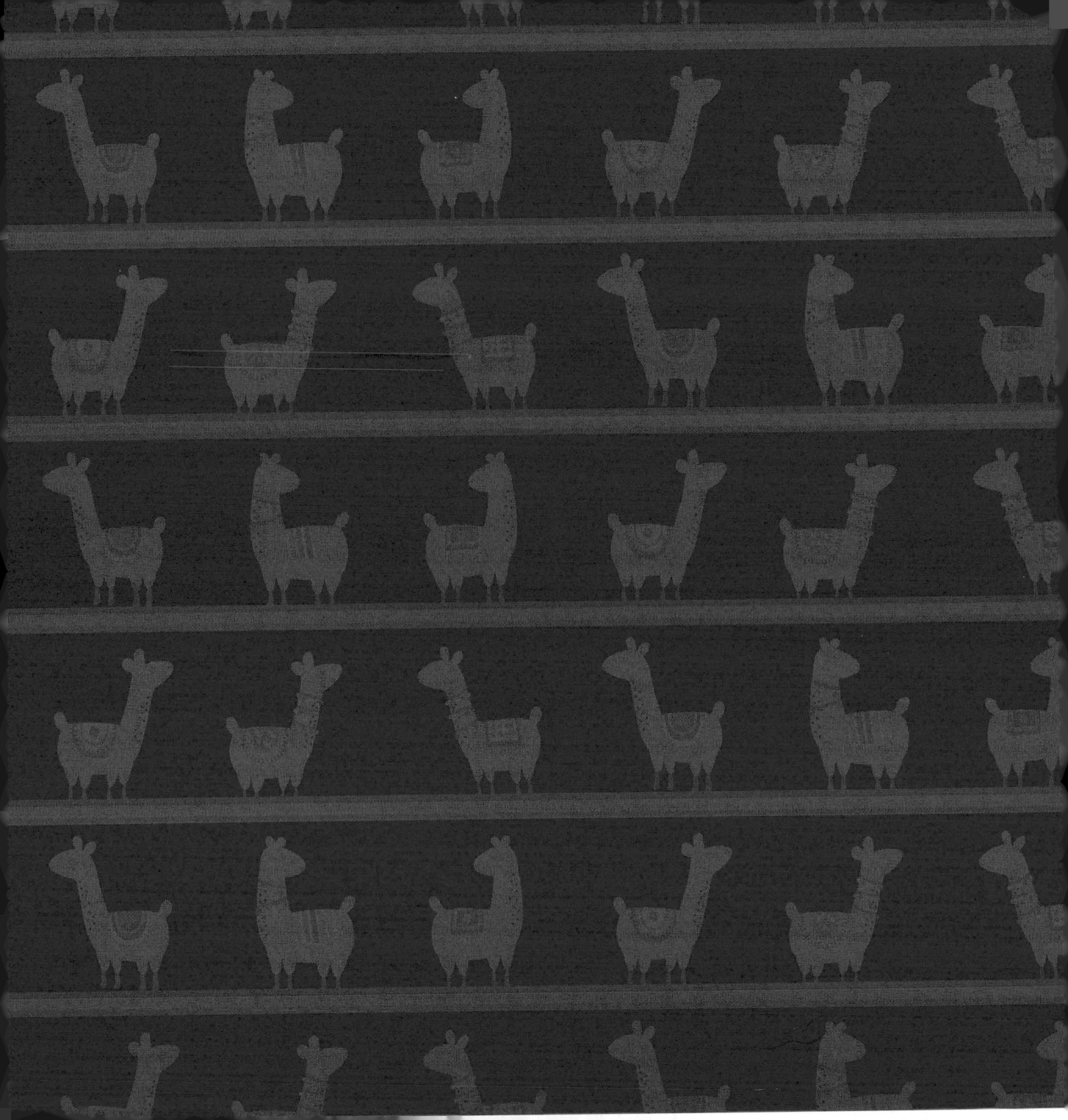

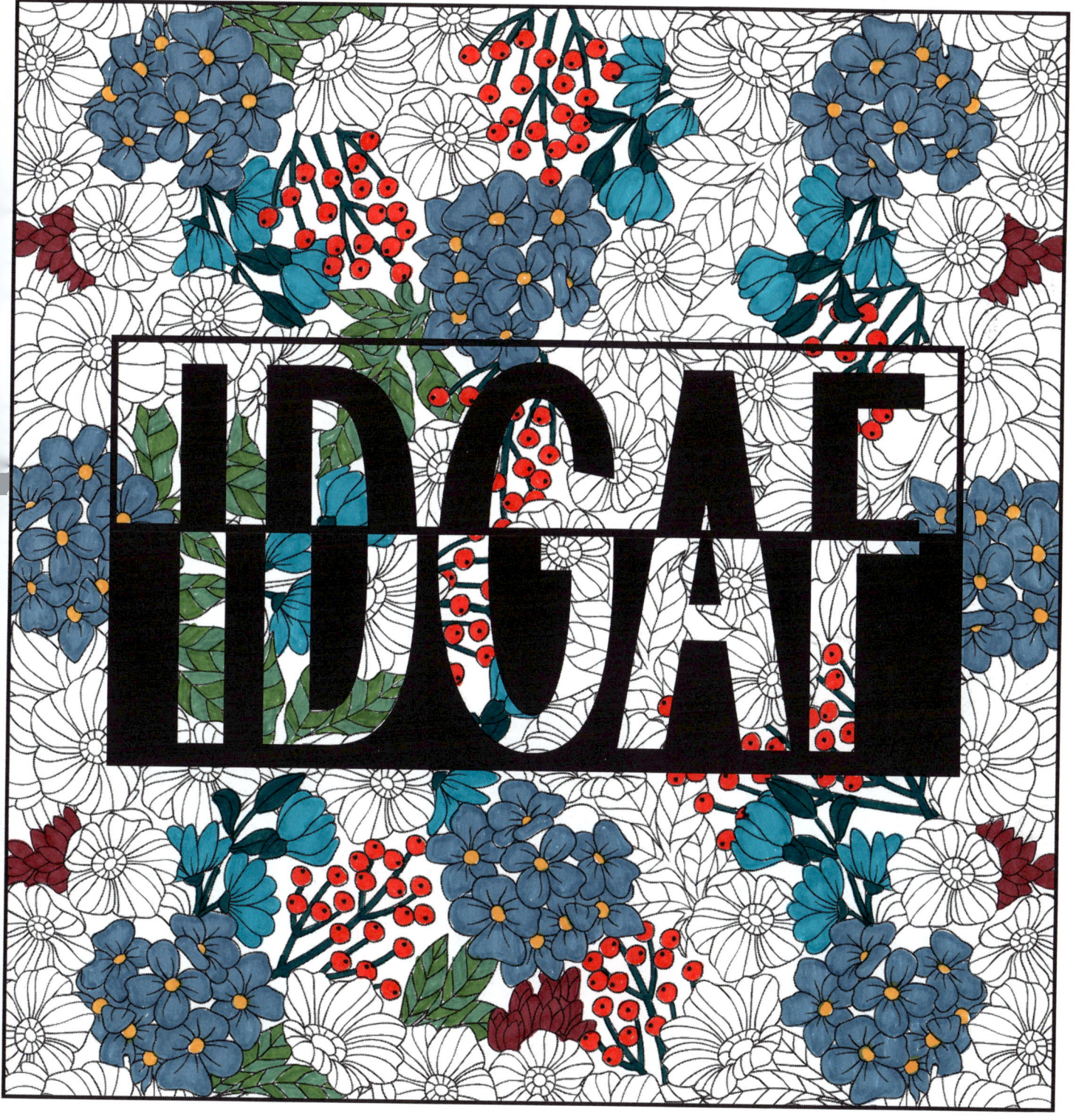

No Fucks given

Don't be such a cock

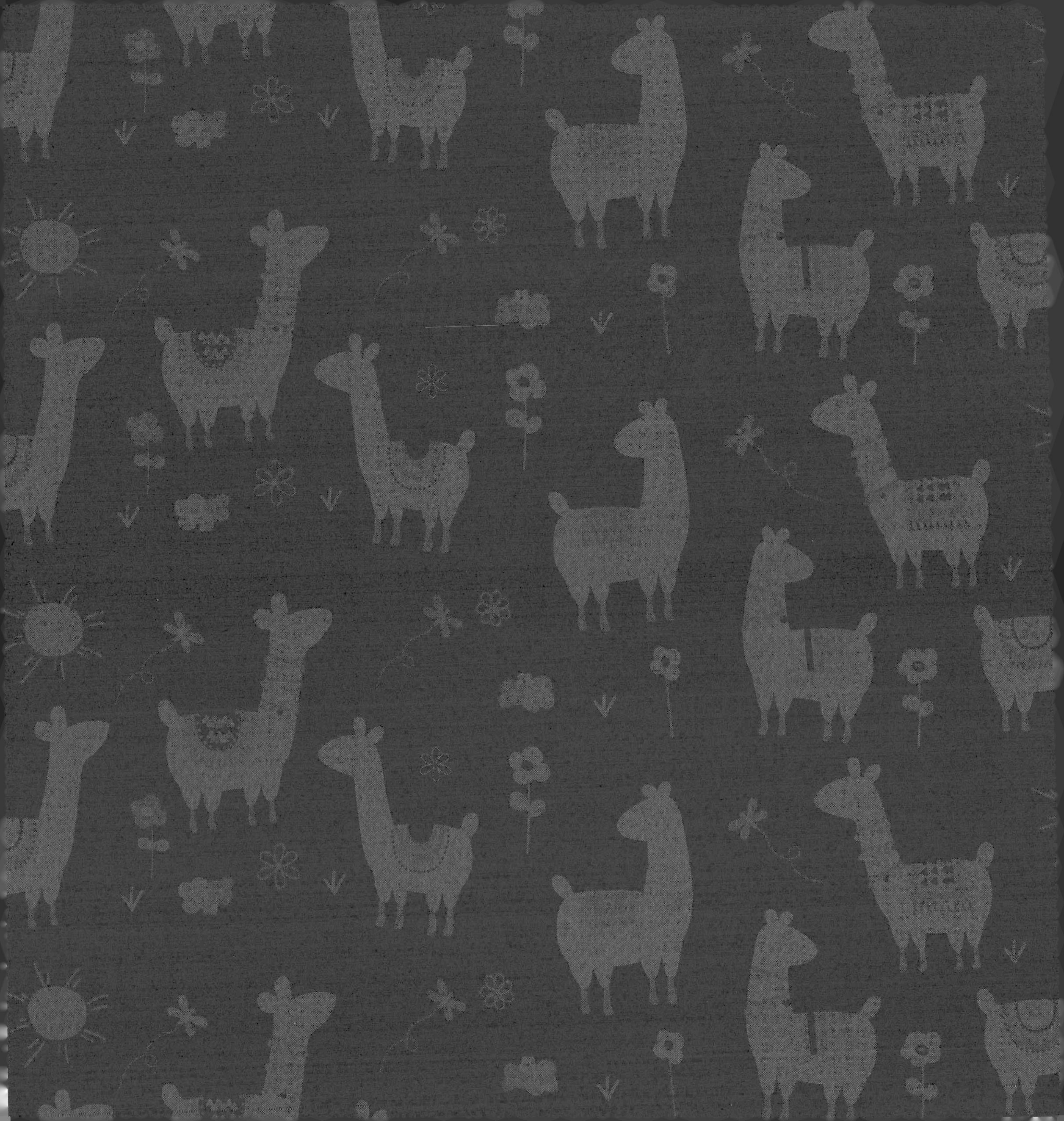

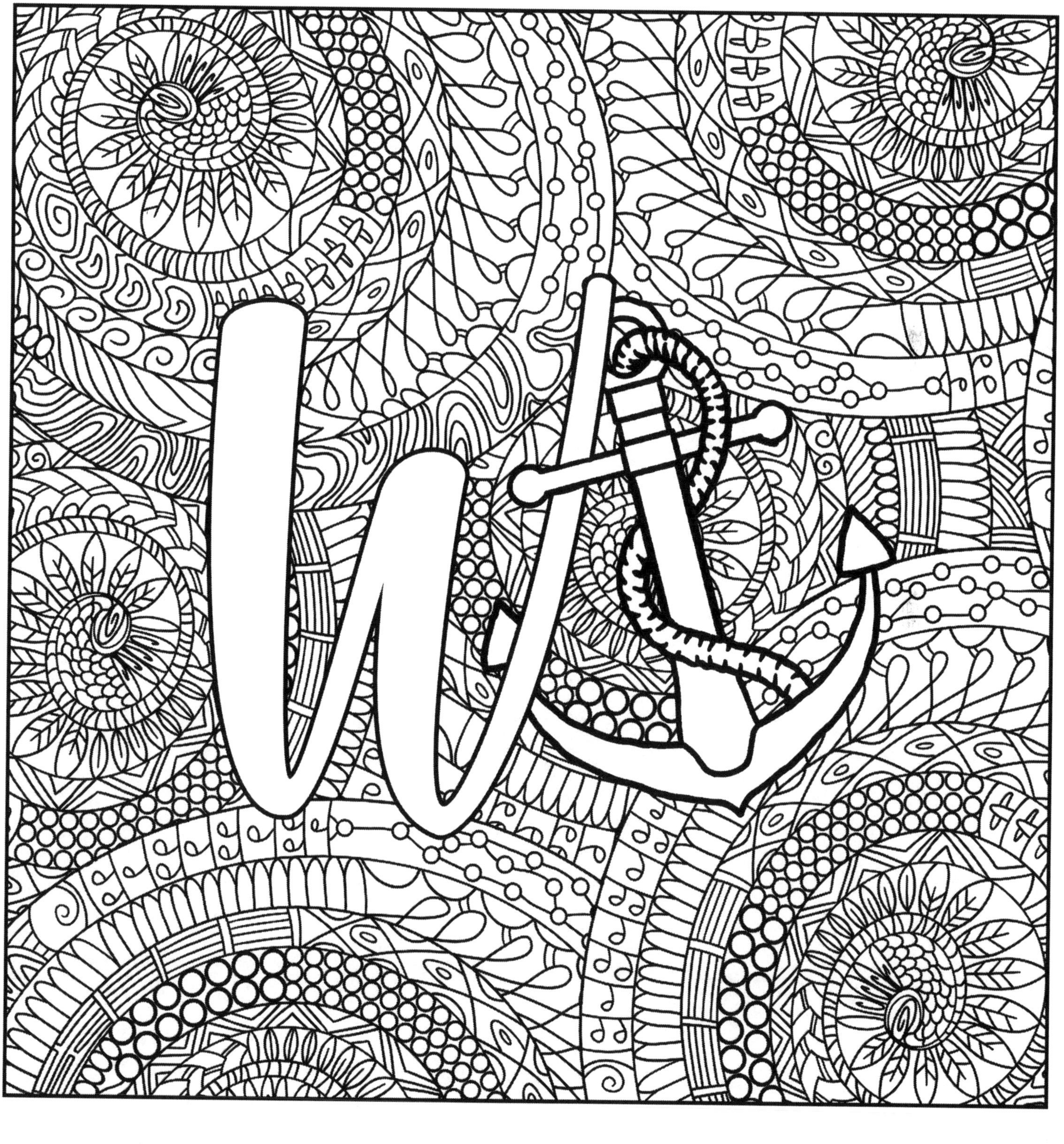
W

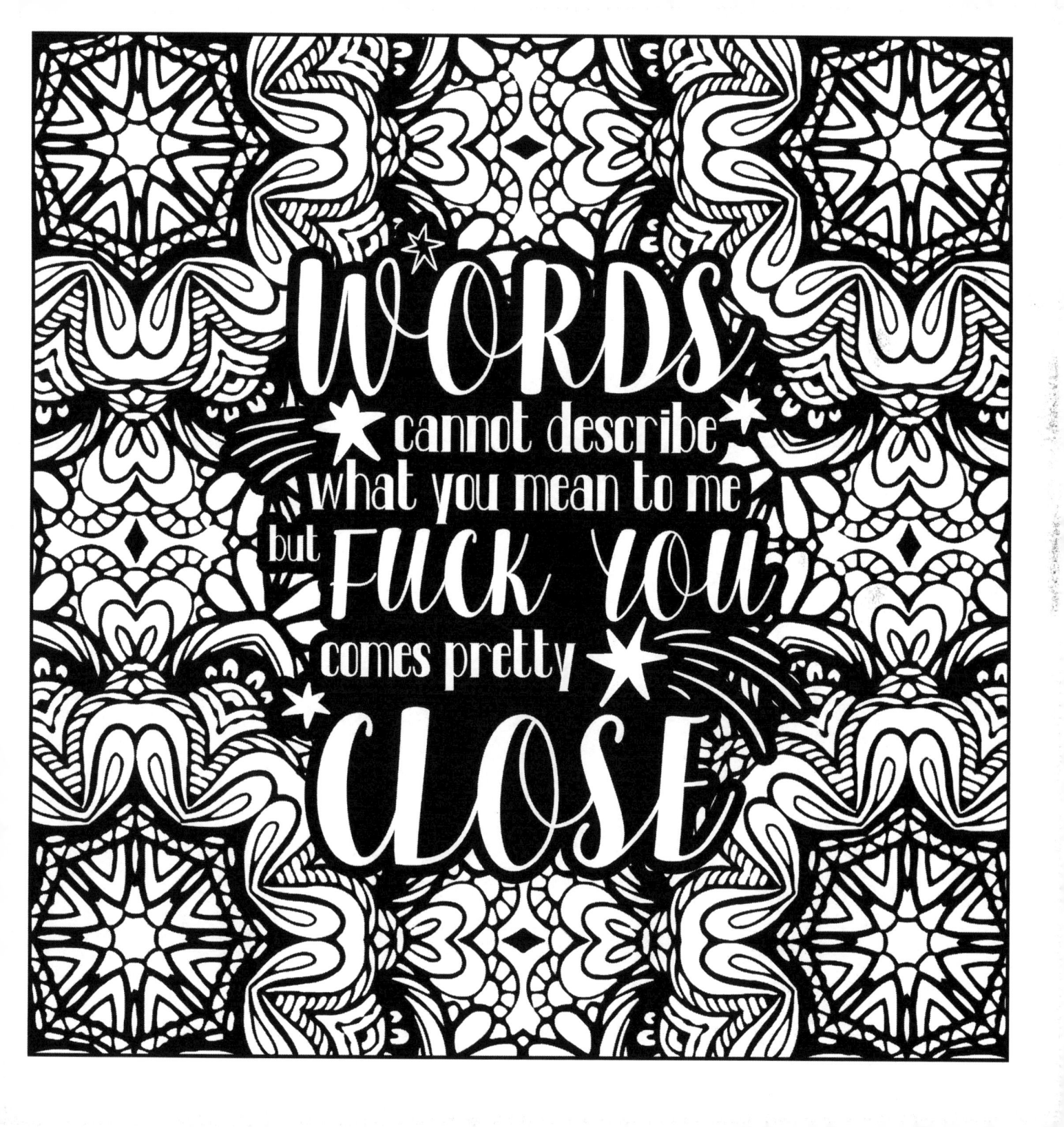

WORDS cannot describe what you mean to me but **FUCK YOU** comes pretty **CLOSE**

Betch

MAMA needs a MOTHER FUCKING nap

No More Fuckery

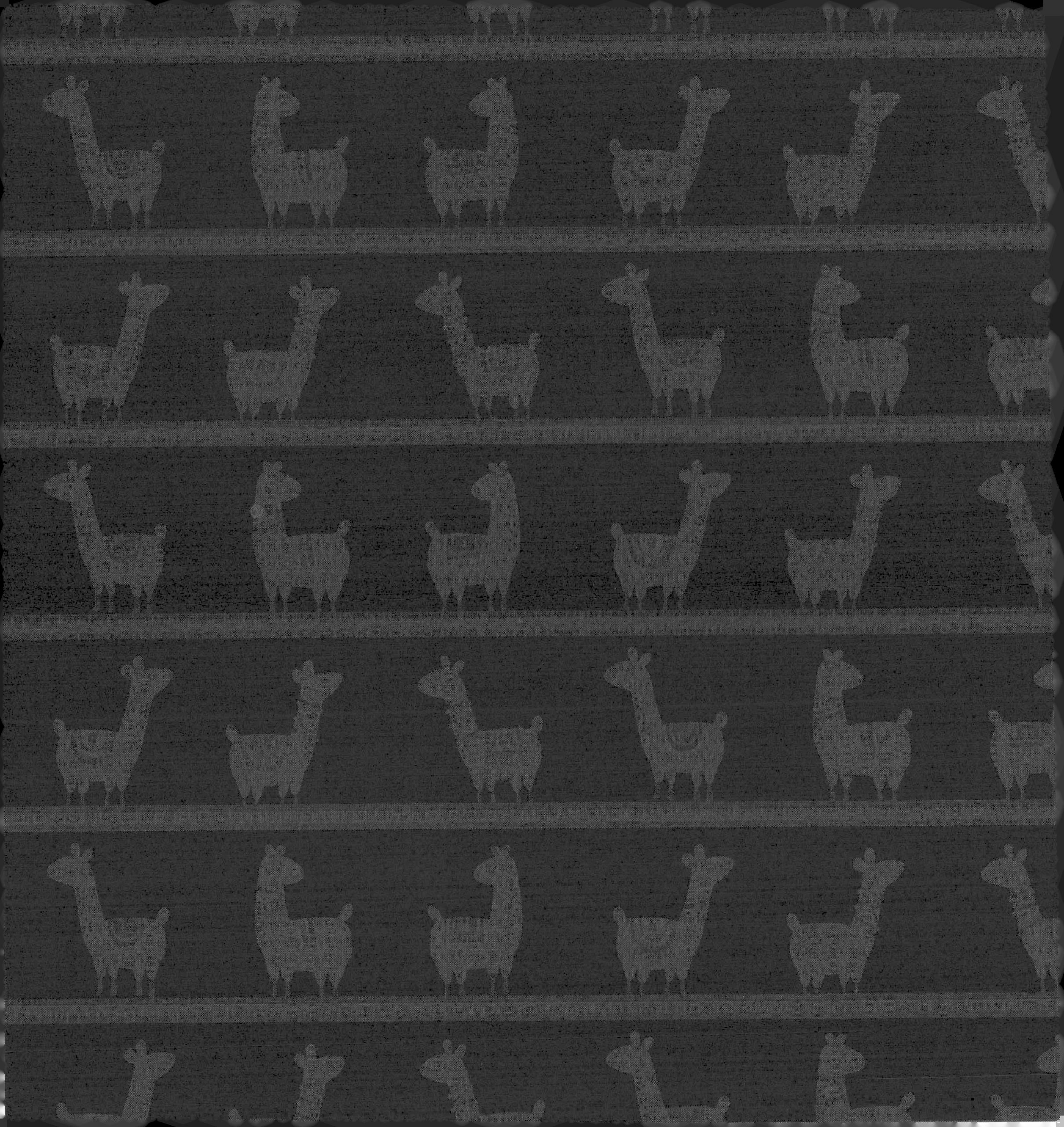

It's a joke, not a dick. Don't take it so hard.

F U
C K

My spirit animal has rabies.

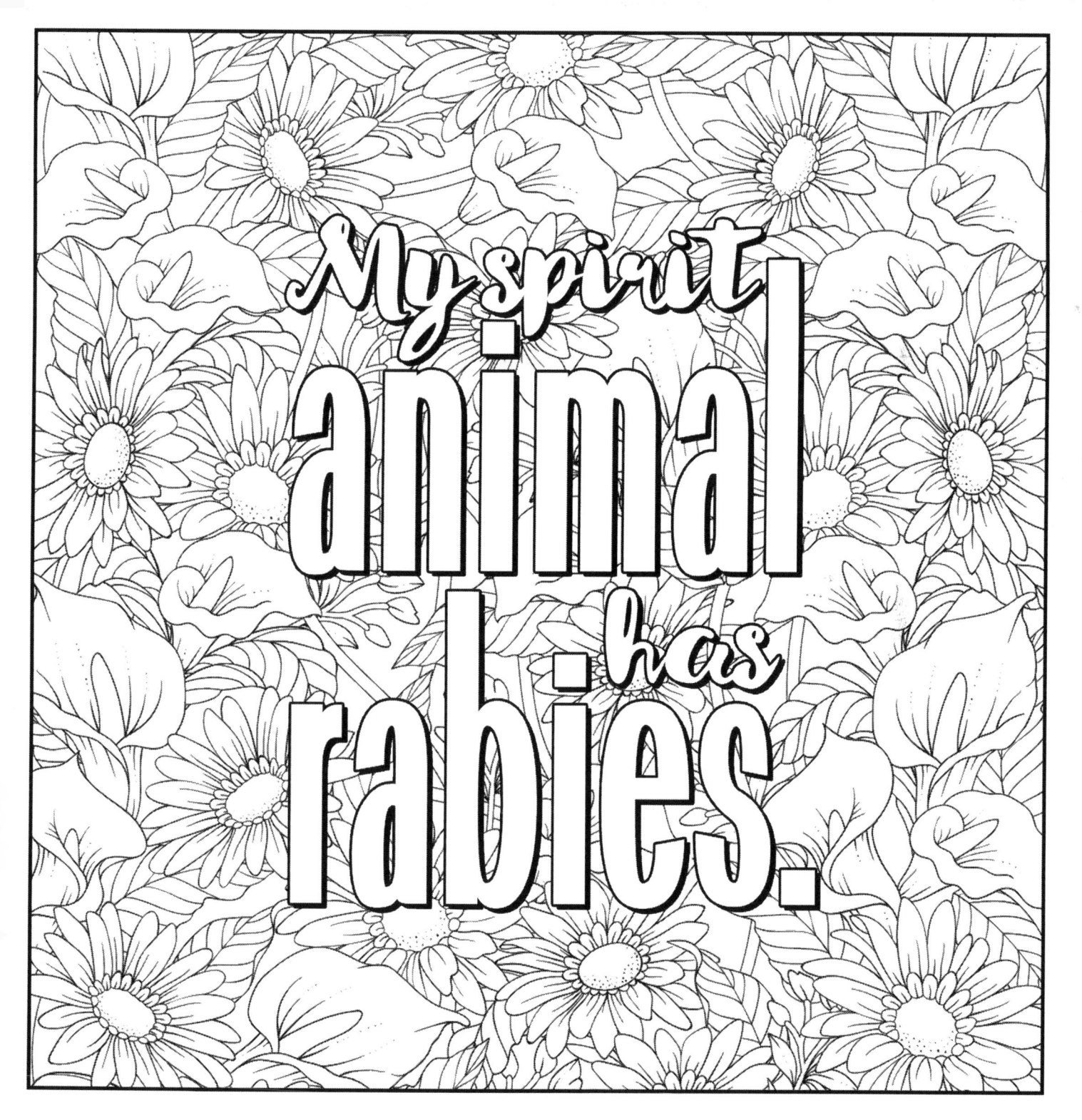

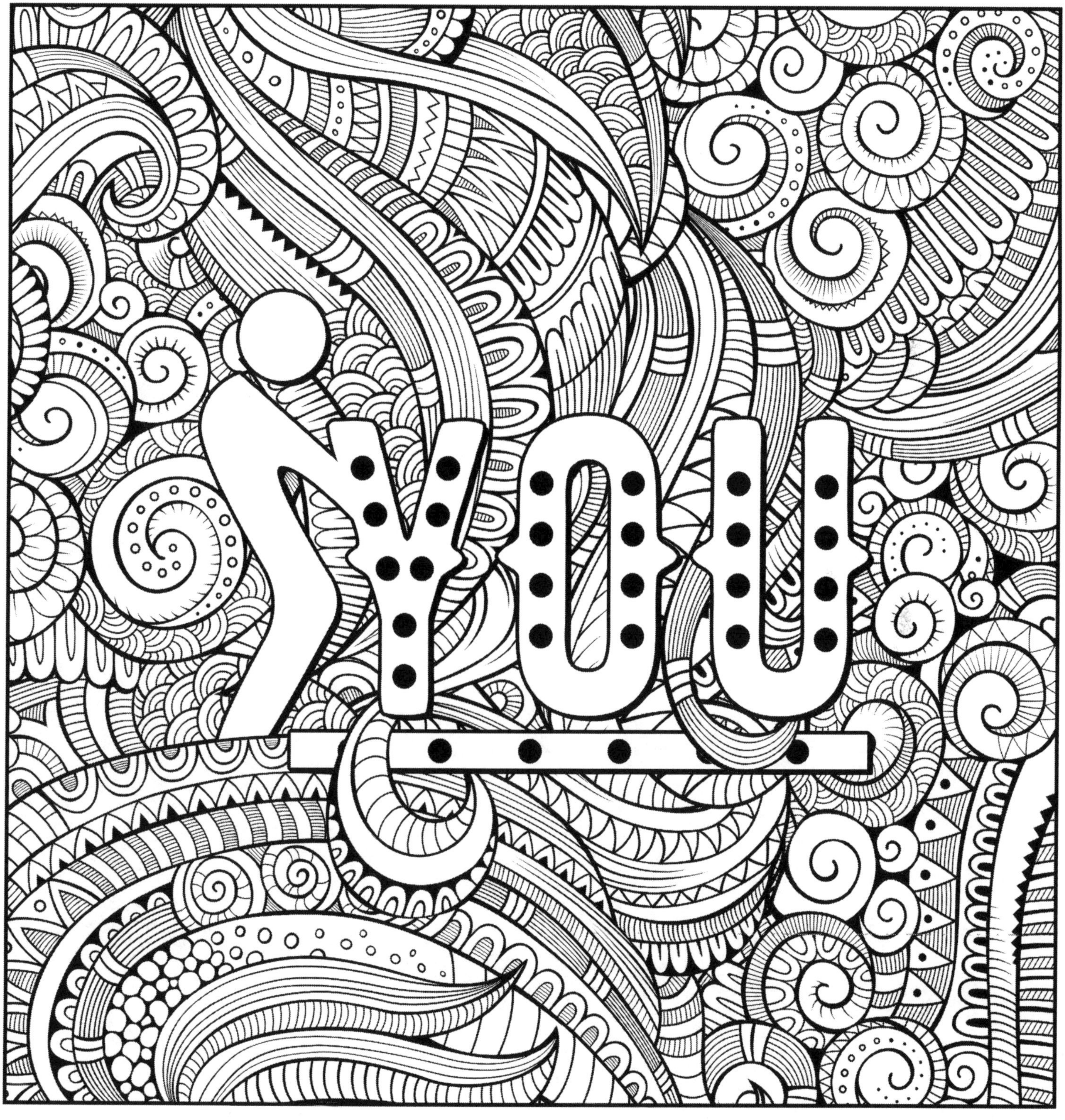
YOU

I've come to the point in my life where I need a stronger word than fuck

Fucky McFuckface

GOEST & FUCKETH THYSELF

Fuck Off

Fresh out of fucks

BE SURE TO FOLLOW US
ON SOCIAL MEDIA FOR THE
LATEST GIVEAWAYS & DISCOUNTS

@honeybadgercoloring

Honey Badger Coloring

@badgercoloring

ADD YOURSELF TO OUR MONTHLY
NEWSLETTER FOR FREE DIGITAL
DOWNLOADS AND DISCOUNT CODES

www.honeybadgercoloring.com/newsletter

CHECK OUT OUR OTHER BOOKS!

www.honeybadgercoloring.com

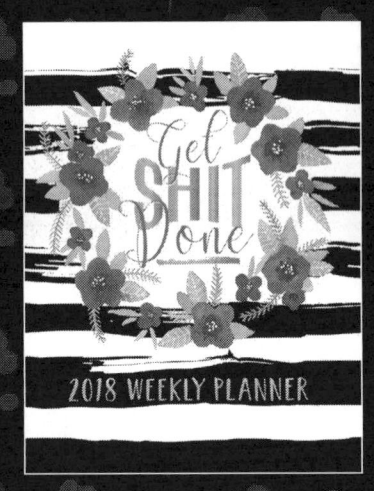

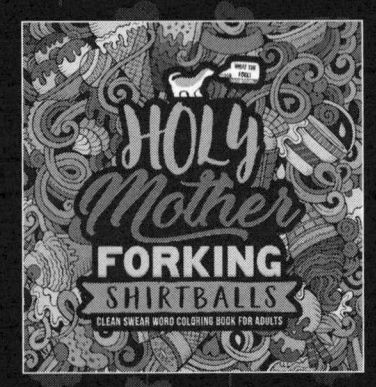

CHECK OUT OUR OTHER BOOKS!

www.honeybadgercoloring.com

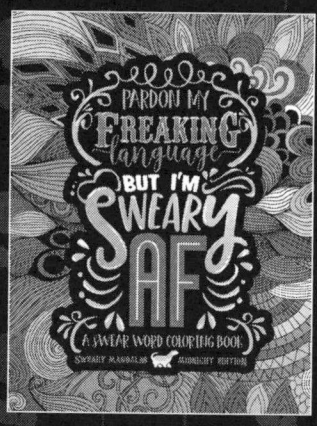

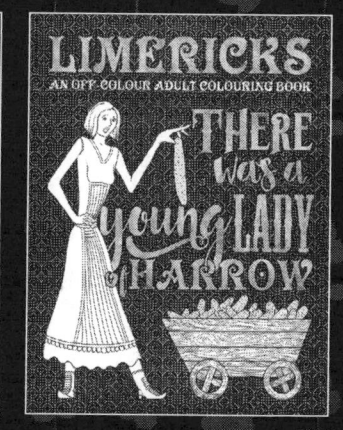

CHECK OUT OUR OTHER BOOKS!

www.honeybadgercoloring.com

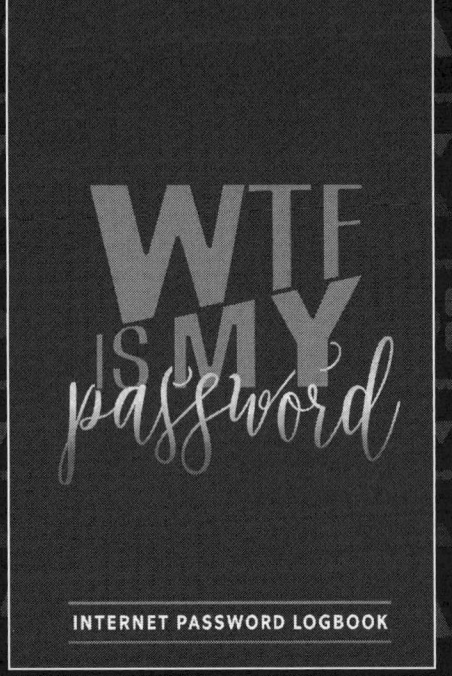

WTF IS MY password
INTERNET PASSWORD LOGBOOK

SHIT I NEED TO REMEMBER
INTERNET PASSWORD LOGBOOK

FREE DOWNLOAD!

www.honeybadgercoloring.com/fresh

YOUR DOWNLOAD CODE: FF3928

@honeybadgercoloring

Honey Badger Coloring